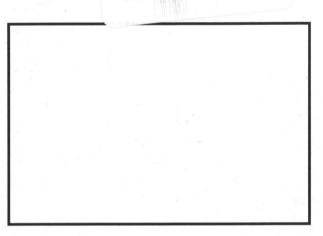

Imperial Nostalgias

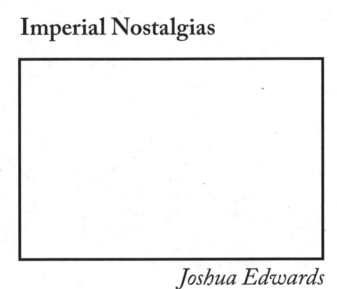

Joshua Edwards

Ugly Duckling Presse
Brooklyn, New York

Imperial Nostalgias
Copyright 2013 by Joshua Edwards
ISBN 978-1-933254-86-9

First Edition, First Printing
Ugly Duckling Presse
232 Third Street #E303, Brooklyn, NY 11215
uglyducklingpresse.org

Distributed by SPD/Small Press Distribution
1341 Seventh Street, Berkeley, CA 94710
spdbooks.org

Cover photograph: "Canopy" (2011) by John Alexander
jrajrajra.com

Design by Don't Look Now!
Typeset in Caslon

Covers printed offset at Polyprint Design
Books printed on recycled paper and bound
at McNaughton & Gunn
Edition of 1000

Support for this publication was provided by
the National Endowment for the Arts

NATIONAL
ENDOWMENT
FOR THE ARTS

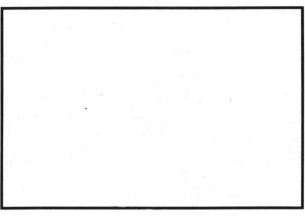

for Lynn

Contents

TWO PARABLES
THE TRAVELER   13
THE OUTSIDER   14

VALLEY OF UNREST   19

DEPARTURES   35

IMPERIAL NOSTALGIAS
SCIENCE VS. LUCK   51
SEASONAL JOB   52
COLD TRAVEL   53
CATHAY   54
THE HEART IS ON THE LEFT SIDE   55
FOR A FOLDING CARD   56
THOMAS JEFFERSON'S CABBAGE   57
IMPERIAL NOSTALGIAS   58
GUESTS   59
ROMANCE   60
SKETCH FOR A TREATISE ON EROS   61
MIDLAND EGRESS   63
PROBLEMS OF KNOWLEDGE   64

STATE OF THE UNION 65

GARDEN OF PERSPECTIVES 66

PRIDE AND ANGER 67

MILITARY FAREWELL 68

FROM THE BOTTOM OF THE STAIRS 70

CROMWELL OR THE KING 71

DEATH IN THE TROPICS 72

A POETICS 73

MONTE ALBÁN 75

FUGITIVE PIECES 81

ACKNOWLEDGMENTS 93

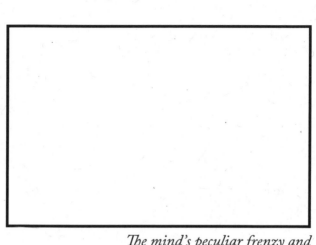

The mind's peculiar frenzy and
The oblivion of things that were
— Lucretius

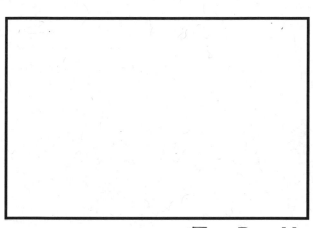

Two Parables

The Traveler

After traveling for many days, the man arrived in the town square and sat down with his legs under him. He spoke and a crowd gathered. He said that the kingdom smelled good and was strong, but that evil was more powerful than ever and had only ducked down out of sight. The crowd listened, jerking forward and buzzing like a swarm of bees.

The man said the people thought of pleasure as their final state, and he called this belief profane. They looked him over. He had a face like a doctor from another country, and they could tell he had spent his life in perpetual hunger. They knew that he could see through the pain that enclosed their lives, like an animal without any mind.

They sat and watched and listened as he issued severe and careful restrictions and spoke, as if reading from a scroll, the names of their most precious ancestors. When he was done speaking, he rose and left town, continuing down the same road he arrived on.

The Outsider

In the dog days, an outsider stuck the real up into the imaginary while standing on a stage, backlit by fireworks, then his body seemed to dissect itself, and at first this display of magic erased the crowd's worst memories of the recent evenings that ruined their city.

But then it seemed as if nobody had heard of the imagination, and after their initial surprise, the people yelled out against the fraudulent showman, saying they would use brute force, threatening to cut his throat. He yelled back at them, "Healing requires... nay, demands a falsification of perspective! I am more real when I sleep than you people are when you're awake!"

This did not sit well with the crowd. Horror, disgust, and then bloodlust filled them, and they surged forward to take hold of the magician, but just as they reached him, he disappeared in a cloud of smoke, leaving behind a note that read, "The next disaster is just around the corner."

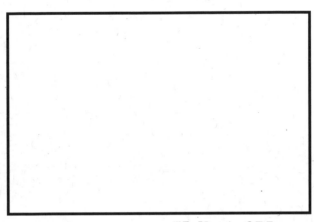

Valley of Unrest

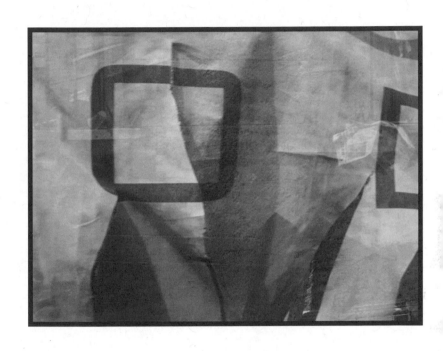

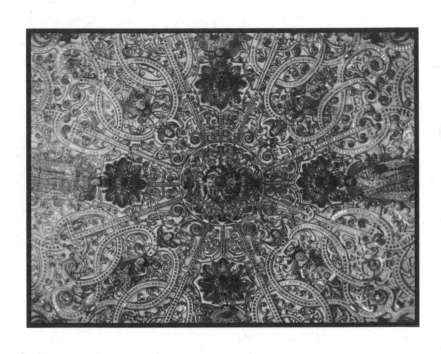

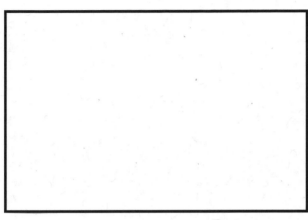

Departures

Underway in a slightly foreign land,
I'm glad to have traveler's air about me,
to be another streak of color exhilarated
and speeding up. Is life movement?
Or a target I'll always be closing in on?
On a journey I become my questions.

*

Such as: If travel is an enemy to ends,
why do they share so many smells and
arrangements? Here there are no
belts of daffodils, just crowds trapped
in margins of stale air on this anniversary
of Abraham Lincoln's assassination.

*

The proportions of the land increase as
the train passes chains of lakefront condos.
Then, from north to west, all trees retreat
to two lines, a football field's width apart.
I'll deeply sleep tonight, played out like this
worn-out farmland, too young for so much wear.

*

Canals make appearances, and the lake
returns briefly. The farms get small and close.
I see a derelict sailboat that could
be a lawn ornament or a divorce
settlement. Welcome to our province.
Violence always starts on the inside.

*

Welcome to spring, I whisper to myself.
To know the punitive damage of all punch
lines is the sorrow of the comic. What
are poets to do with the silence they put
their poems into? It's difficult to imagine
having a heart attack in this country.

*

The last thing I see of the largest city
in this kingdom is a billboard depicting
a sports car and a caption, "Careful,
envy is a sin." I remember when reverse
psychology seemed so cool to me,
I thought Buddha must have invented it.

*

Now I hear the Majjhima Patipada
promoted in my favorite beer commercial,
first aired at half-time during last year's
Super Bowl, on a day like every day, a day
to say grace and give thanks for a brain
and the cans that I can crush against it.

*

The ride gets too rough for my weary eyes
so instead of reading I daydream. My
name is starting to seem too serious.
I try to remember what it felt like
to be accompanied by someone else,
en route somewhere, in a nowhere like here.

*

I read. "The word at rest rests in the mind
in the restless continuation." "The interruption
of persistent locomotion." *I* is a word
at rest, resting in the mind. I am my own
interruption, the location of one locution on
this locomotive. Thank you, Robert Duncan.

*

Beware the claptrap. Full sounds emanate
from damaged lives. However, this vigor
is the means to a nice vacation home
or a heart attack. Romanticism,
dinner, sadism, salad, and desert:
things that will change over the border.

*

Out the right window, the lake, blue and white,
resembles the ocean, without such depth.
Swans, blackbirds, a small town, its factory,
and an awful stench come and go, avec
politesse. A man holds his daughter's hand
and they wave to whomever they see pass.

*

The approaching language frontier smells like
beef stew. Or should I think beef bourguignon?
When I do enter ambiguity
it will become clear to me just how long
it is I have been gone for. Until then,
I'll watch birds and chew my bottom lip.

*

Prostitutes gather on the hotel stoop
tonight, beneath this dark window. The line
is fine between lust's excitement and love's
indictment. I recollect all the times
I fell in love with pain I thought was cute.
Knock, knock. "Veux-tu m'emporter dans ta chute?"

*

Room 209 is small and simple: bed,
chair, lamp, two mirrors, sink (certainly pissed
in before because the john's down the hall),
gas radiator, and a ceiling fan
that helps to heighten the hotel's diction.
Knock, knock. "Veux-tu m'emporter dans ta chute?"

*

What I desire most is to rest easy
despite knowing what will happen to life.
On television, the sexomercials
commence. No emancipation without
that of society. Lights off. TV?
Knock, knock. "Veux-tu m'emporter dans ta chute?"

*

The first show I see at the Musée des
beaux-arts is photography that examines,
perhaps, deviation and loneliness.
Then I go see paintings, two of which
are tame John Currins. Two more, wild
and fresh, are by Massimo Guerrera.

*

The next room I enter is large and filled
with big art. It even smells valuable.
Mario Merz's glass sculpture, *Triplo Igloo*,
is central. It's surrounded by six giant
paintings. The only kinship I notice is
their scale. I prefer the frantic Richter.

*

In a building that will soon be destroyed,
I wake up and drink tea, then relax
on my friend's couch to watch *Paris, Texas*
for the first time. When someone goes silent,
or when a sibling is filled with sorrow,
the whole world resembles a motel room.

*

Though elegant by nature, this country
has become indelicate and ugly
in many spaces. Severe déjà vu
precedes an abrupt loss of memory
for a place that believes itself to be
both paradigmatic and distinctive.

*

A boy and his father walking home from
school on opposite sides of a street then
meeting in the middle reflects their life
together, their language and affliction.
They enter a car together to search
for the source of mutual consciousness.

*

I talk to myself about sex. How sad.
I pat myself on the back to dislodge
the extra voice caught in my throat. Some nights
I'm as calm as the Moon, but not tonight.
I crave sleep and am annoyed by the Moon,
the Pleiades, the Big Dipper, and Mars.

*

The capital emits the nightmare of
a man whose hollow leg is packed with
explosives. The irony, of course, is
that he wears the prosthetic because he
lost his leg to a landmine, fighting for
the freedom of those he now wants to kill.

*

To create actual violence out
of diplomatic anger requires an
indulgence to the spirit of pity
and the monument of pain. Intercourse
between governments is trash talk in which
the trash is memos about ballistics.

*

Viewing time as a series of actions,
one must intercede with appropriate
enthusiasm. Sometimes, this calls for
a change in weight class. Others, it requires
hiring a third party to strike the knee
of a competitor with a baton.

*

All my words are written down in black on
white, documentary-style, but my self
is nothing if not fictive, easily
addicted to wishes for what's not true.
My political engagement consists
of questionable associations.

*

I have formulated a new type of
resistance, against my own ignorance:
I transplant my mind a few times a day,
replacing it with unreliable
algorithms aimed at solving problems,
known as poems. I call them *departures*.

*

"An entomologist is not a bug,"
is what Rexroth said to sever his ties
with the Beats. Almost all criticism
is like traveling by train, then saying
you've seen the world. Everyone knows that all
you've seen is the shit that's around the tracks.

*

All music's subtext is forgiveness, right?
And I wonder what type songs I should write.
A good starting point would be Adorno's
statement, "Distance is not a safety zone
but a field of tension." Isn't that the truth…
I submit failed relationships as proof.

*

Passing beneath southern stars, I think
of kudzu, my alien nation, roads to hell.
The natural world creates analogy
for human technology where the two
merge, but nobody seems to give a fuck.
Where forests meet fields, I observe deer blinds.

*

I must admit I don't understand
nature, or how an author can insert
it into a creed, but I know nothing
about gardens or decomposition.
If *hello* is the forest and *goodbye*
is the field, then where is *superego*?

*

I reread Yvor Winters's passage about
childhood and reverie, the search for some
release, until I know it by heart. I look out
at the land's incommensurable peace. In
some places, ours seems such a simple age.
I think of this scenery as a turned page.

*

At my favorite museum, I stare at some
notable art, like Hans Haacke's *Blue Sail*,
Rauschenberg's *Erased de Kooning Drawing*,
Narkissos by Jess, Toba Khedoori's *Untitled*,
Georgia O'Keeffe's *Black Place I*, and
Michael Jackson and Bubbles by Jeff Koons.

*

A photography exhibit, *Beyond Real*, contrasts
surrealist and contemporary photos, with
boring results. The exceptions are Claude
Cahun's self-portraits and *New York* by Helen
Levitt. Also, Hiroshi Sugimoto's work, which
reminds me of home without associations.

*

The cows outside will be slaughtered and
workers will separate what's edible from
refuse. This changes the landscape's tone.
If I knew all the facts, I would most likely
never open my mouth. It's Mother's Day.
The planet Earth smells awfully human.

*

The way nature is forgotten haunts
outdoor funeral services, where bodies
lying in state lose their anthropological
appeal. They instead become studies
of conclusion without repercussion.
They become absolute futurist losers.

*

Today I woke up with a floating thought,
"Undermining one's own authority
is the new black." Maybe that means something,
probably not. Last night I had a dream
about death and mourning, and a speedboat.
I strain to make the connection with love.

*

Perhaps love rests within relationships
as an intoxicated question that
surfaces and is passed around from one
drinker to another, until the warmth
of personhood approaches violence
and language gives way to telepathy.

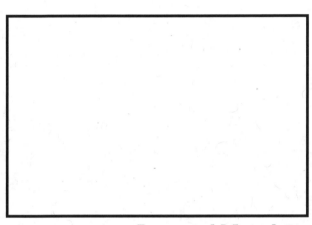

Imperial Nostalgias

Science vs. Luck

Specters are haunting a fair afternoon in the common ruin.

All that is holy is profaned by a fire the neighbors have made in fear.

General phases go on as the living undress at night.

An enormous dog was killed and lay near the battle.

This animal is the misery of a river whose water is the course of time.

Unbelief in a common language rolls back the wheel of history.

Bodies of the deceased do away with a form of property.

Waves toss simple articles of a small, inferior sea.

Seasonal Job

Working in a mountain's shadow, for a manager whose
will is a mirror, how you walk and where are the only
forms of amusement outside your mind, which seems
complete and complicated, but when studied wants rework.

Although you have a sense of time, you don't consider how
long it will take to prepare. In other words, you never know
if you should leave or even if you can. This is the era when
autumn is everything, and the only proof of this is autumn.

Cold Travel

Black bough
against dusk

(for steadily
growing up)

once again
to observe

border towns
clover fields

famous people
covered in frost.

Cathay

Wrongheaded and obsequious
on vacation, unnerved
by new surroundings, I miss
the bright feeling of belonging
and the familiar patterns of my country,
its virginity and schizophrenia,
my several stolen bicycles.

The Heart Is on the Left Side

Revolvers evoke cemeteries in
which visual symbols are supposed to
be obvious and simple. Clearly they
are only invitations to affix

to language the significance of the
emotions that arise between a verb
and its object. Symbolic gestures feel
bound not by referential expression,

but by mystery and drama. If all
languages are essentially alike,
then softness or firmness is a matter
of tissues in which blood takes a clausal

complement. Taste for etymology,
however, comes from the poetry of
crucial decision making, fruit in one
hand and broad-bladed knife in the other.

For a Folding Card

There's gold
in the Pharaoh's rectum.

The mouth of the Queen
is loaded with rose petals.

The Emperor's eyes
have been replaced by myrrh.

For all the holes
in sky and earth: filling.

In each orifice:
an offering.

On every envelope addressed
to whatever: a stamp.

Thomas Jefferson's Cabbage

The sightseers know what they are seeing, for it is written
on the signs. This plantation, surrounded by slave gardens
and full of ghosts, is pretty as a picture. Using Benjamin
Banneker's almanac, one could ascertain the best cure
for a mild rash or which night of 1792 would be most
perfect for reading the works of Machiavelli by moonlight.

"All states, all powers that have held and hold rule over
 men…"

Imperial Nostalgias

They tried to prove,
through enterprise and art,
that a journey's end exists
at the outset, as a darkened lamp
that tumbles back through
all the stages of its building
into a dream of light.

Guests

I welcome my friends.
They visit in the winter to get warm
or to be somewhere new or to escape
from someone
or something that happened.
I'm glad to play host, to show them
the common pleasures of a place.
We invoke old questions about home.
We discuss relationships.
We walk.
We celebrate landscape, deride technology,
and try to keep other foreigners
out of our photographs, except for
the ones meant to show
how much stranger than us
other foreigners must be.

Romance

To be in a relationship could mean
to be a whole world discrete,
and that's the danger. For example:
a person might point out that Friedrich
Hölderlin looks like George Washington
in some paintings. It seems a reasonable
enough remark, but because the other
person cares for Hölderlin so much more
than Washington (or vice versa) it starts
a fight; likewise the simple subject of food
or how someone talks about money
during sex. The labyrinth of another's
understanding can be so painful, it may
carry with it the risk of myth and provoke
the unsuccess of which it warns.

Sketch for a Treatise on Eros

There is of course to be in love
but also how to be sane and not
annoy the beloved or belittle them.
At their best, two people may

destroy certain barricades and
like a map folded into the shape
of an airplane, set out toward
a place that wasn't there before.

After sitting together for hours
for the first time, they may emerge
from their talk into a world more
like the one they'd wanted, as if

they had somehow been together
all along, when they weren't.
They're changed as if the past
itself had changed. They've traded

old burdens for desire's oppression.
A description of love could be
people making decisions together
and the beautiful danger of that.

Midland Egress

Formally studying the mind's eye,
they sit feeling very alive at humble
desks to compose mesmeric songs
with damaged hearts. They hallucinate
for transformative texts, which they
improve by dreaming up eternal readers.
The horizon empties of classic themes
and foreign lights shine on everything.

Problems of Knowledge

Translation broadens language
as divorce and remarriage extend family.

Born to fade and break, facts
huddle inside black brackets.

Work means inquisition as a child
separates a cricket's wings from thorax.

Ideas come apart as monads, metastasizing
rhapsody on the edge of delicate dusk.

Thunder sounds in the distance or television,
always on in this constant rain.

State of the Union

The song of our green-eyed family
is a song about the bread we bake.

Snow comes down and misfortune
closes its hands around our necks.

I cannot read to my children until
the roses my husband bought me wilt.

Sunlight no longer plays on the river
and heaven is black beyond compare.

Garden of Perspectives

Whenever your hands resemble question marks,
whenever you try to open a jar for someone and
can't or wake up grasping at what, in that moment,

you sense can barely be held at all, you go outside
to employ a shovel or a rake. There in the garden,
where the stilted increments of life are only a vague

buzz easily ignored among the flowers, you comb
and stab the earth, while your attention slowly turns
from the lightning of birth to the thunder of death.

Pride and Anger

When it breaks
something else
mostly gets broken.

Almost over with the year,
it is empty.
Frame-wrecked and windblown.

*

What is lost
moves in across the street,
another
object of desire.

They drain the pool
for winter.

Military Farewell

Various groups talk about motion
and the motion of a life
getting in the way,
what an underarm
stain is to the ocean of effort.

(Alas, child asleep.)

*

They are almost the same, but whose
flowers and whose activity?

*

Ambition.
A small love letter
within a request
for a change in love
and in the center of that
(*Bam! Bam!*), the noise
of something falling
following the sound
of what makes it fall.

From the Bottom of the Stairs

The woman's voice rises as a harsh song,
while upstairs the man reverses aging
with a balm then wipes his forehead

with a kerchief. The day is warm until
three calls saying: the neighbor's child
was bitten, is allergic, has passed away.

They are so sad they reset the table with
paper dishes and a flower that could never
hold any bee's attention. The day gathers

the couple in its hull and blows a horn.
The air fills with a notion to hold still and
they hold air still within, as though time

were something that leaks from lungs
and not some thing that whispers as
it passes first closely and then away.

Cromwell or the King

In the European fog, one startled
while another rests and resting waits
for heavy closure. Philosophy, the lion's
dark maw, changes seasons. The nation's

ring of war regains renown: crowns,
new necks, and talent for violating
weakness. You want to paint the world
you were born into, but when you try

you're only able to portray this one
that will kill you. You can't get the oils
to impasto right, and the dried-blood red
you desire doesn't seem to exist anymore.

Death in the Tropics

The parrots will squawk
whatever was whispered.

A Poetics

The reflections of fables return
in the bloody search for truth as
the frightening power of breathing.

A lover's fine sense of crises is never
far from the body nor from culture—
melancholy lust of the human world.

It all seems part of a series of works
less thoughtless than life, but not as clear,
like a journey between exhaustion and joy.

This journey, both visual and corporeal,
can only be established with imagery,
and this is also true of a shoemaker.

Living in the forest's heart, his drama
stands for the storms and solitude
of winter as cosmos molds mankind.

The universe comes to inhabit his house,
the solid representation of which is folded
as time is impregnated with unreality.

A mind increases majesty as the theme
of closing doors grows sharper and
two strangers exchange images.

Since images are more demanding than
ideas, a critic will probably ask if only
the bird building its nest is content.

Monte Albán

I

On this high ledge it seems history's
indeterminate plans and resolutions
compete for what little space is left
in the graveyard. When I was young
civilization seemed the most accurate
word to describe my surroundings.

Many years later I learned about
World War II, Albert Speer, and
the phantasmagoria of the theory
of Ruin Value. It broke my spirit.
Now, surrounded by pyramids
in a valley bereft of panthers, still

disappointed in people and gods,
alone with a thousand years of silence,
I think of Kenneth Patchen fighting
with pain for the occupation of his
mind as he writes, "This is my life,
Caesar. / I think it is good to live."

II

Through a turnstile, past a diorama
of ruins, into the ruins themselves.
Ruins as diorama, ruins as sculpture,
birds as music boxes. Everything
moves toward metaphor and dream.

All the plants have wilted back home,
where dust collects on bookshelves
and covers catalogues, atlases, and
old travel guides. I squint to define
the sun in its place above platforms

and tombs. The imaginary unknown
makes me laugh like an idiot, as I see
my life as a museum visit at the end
of a long vacation. I have lost my way
and now call disorientation paradise.

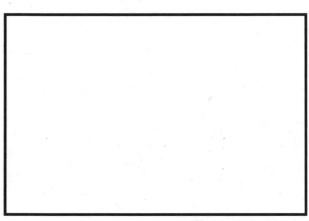

Fugitive Pieces

October boredom making stilts
A tin of candies on the nightstand

To the politician
Destroyer of words
Hydrocarbon suburbia lantern and effete
Are all useless now
Futility alone remains

Dead birds by the sliding glass door
A receipt for sundry items
The life of Lafcadio Hearn in Japan

There are two sides to everything
One sticks out its chest
The other sticks a knife in its back

To be free again
Moving outward as a space in the trees
Vengeance

An equation for rain and the most terrible
Honeymoon in Texas
Lives were as short
As the longest songs of fondness

The newspaper is crumpled
Around four music boxes

A guitar being played in the foyer ears perked
All night trees made their sounds against the roof
All night the river moved beside the trees

A bird crossed a wide tract of sadness
And tackled its savior into the river

Pain was sticking to the wound
The chicken tasted of train steam
Invaders spilled tea
Hope may die at any moment

An idiomatic expression about skinning a cat
Daylight savings time
A small epidemic against a field of stars

Riding in a hearse
Down the Rue Gît-le-Cœur

Infinitude beats down
On a calming voice

Form is far more patient
Than the hunting rifle of rough desire

Such is loyalty
The past will never testify

A parachute on a high school football field
After rehearsal the choir goes to play in the clay

The flock roams wild without the young shepherd
And the bed of the merchant's daughter is empty

Flesh-colored underwear
In a Protestant graveyard

Hoodwinked by a mainstay and an open position

Potential for change
Remains a fetish economy
In the capable hands
Of a flight instructor

Selling horse teeth
On the black market
Trying desperately
To flatten against the wall
To avoid being seen

A fetish
Is a depressing metaphor

Try burning fruit brother
It will not work
Don't disparage
The world was made for observations

Life is terrible enough without swans

Stranger talking to stranger on the street
One hiding behind a bolo tie
The other behind a long cigarette

Nature gave us horses
The Sierras and glaciers
All of this from a spark
How erotic

With an abacus figuring the turnpike

In Valencia the two-toned hotel
Becomes a home

The cartoon wolf sleeps alone

In the painting is it an apple
A plastic apple
It is a pear

Decorum is always struggling with prosperity
In the cold eternity of pleasure

Acknowledgments

Thanks to the editors of *The Buenos Aires Review*, *Colorado Review*, *LIT*, *Northwest Review*, *Parthenon West Review*, *Practice*, *Slate*, *Smartish Pace*, *The Tiny*, *Tuesday: An Art Project*, *Vanitas*, *Verse*, and *Vert*, where versions of some of these poems and photographs previously appeared.

My deepest gratitude to my family, friends, teachers, and editors for everything. In particular: David Jou, Matvei Yankelevich, Linda Trimbath, and everyone at Ugly Duckling Presse for their vision and support, John Alexander for the perfect cover art, and Lynn Xu for her ideas, edits, and companionship.

Thanks also to the Fulbright-García Robles Program, *Zoland Poetry*, the Vermont Studio Center, the Stegner Program at Stanford University, and the Creative Writing Program and International Institute at the University of Michigan for grants and fellowships that made this work possible.

The title of this book is a taken from a series of poems in César Vallejo's *Los heraldos negros* (*The Black Heralds*).

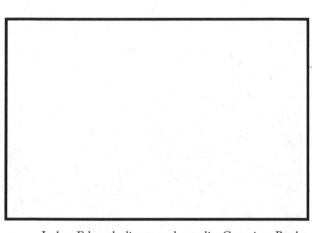

Joshua Edwards directs and co-edits Canarium Books. He is the author of *Campeche* (with photographs by his father, Van Edwards) and the translator of Mexican poet María Baranda's *Ficticia*. He has received fellowships at Akademie Schloss Solitude and the Stegner Program, among other honors.